THE RIGHT TO BIRTH

THE RIGHT TO BIRTH

Sean P. Twomey

A Hearthstone Book

Carlton Press Corp. New York

Manufactured in the United States of America
ISBN 0-8062-5087-9

Dedication

To my wife Ellen, with whom I shared the disappointment of nature's abortions; to our first born, Mary Beth, and our other three children, Shaun, Aileen and Geraldine, who but for failed pregnancies, would not have joined her in gracing our lives.

Acknowledgment

Special thanks to Michele Skowronski, of the Cliffside Park Library, whose cooperation in many areas, but especially in procuring books on feral children, made my research much easier.

Contents

Preface

In the words of one reader: "You've said it all; that's the end of the debate." Although the author states that the aim is not to show that abortion is right or wrong; just that each side allow freedom of conscience to the other, doubt being sufficient for that mental attitude, his argument substantiated by Catholic teaching, leaves no room for doubt; it clearly establishes that the fetus should not be dignified with the inherent rights of human personality.

But should cold reason not prevail against the heat of an emotional wall, a principle is sought whereby, while many remain certain in their own minds that not only abortion, but also other values are evil as well, nevertheless, they will not seek the strong arm of the state to impose their philosophy, but will be happy with the full freedom to expound it; they will confine themselves to using moral force only, not legal.

The cure is democracy, but so far we have failed to read the prescription; once we do so and take the medicine, many of our ills will disappear.

However, there will be many who refuse to abide by democratic principles, who in effect insist on imposing otherworld values through this world government. This attitude was most manifest in the Cairo Population Conference, and is surfacing and threatening to weigh heavily on the debate in the use of fetal-tissue to treat Parkinson's disease. If reconciliation proves impossible, and the lines are clearly drawn between the contending forces of democracy and fundamentalism, in greater or lesser degrees, the challenge perforce must be met. A separation must be devised between those who maintain this world is an end in itself and those for whom it is but a means to a life hereafter. Efforts to confine to its practitioners the consequences of their anti-this-world way of life, are preferable to open confrontation.

Those who opt for a way of life that leads to a population in excess of their ability to provide, must not expect others to heed their cry for help. It is for them to stew in their own juices.

THE RIGHT TO BIRTH

Abortion and the Soul

Nobody will find it illuminating to be told that on the abortion issue there are two diametrically opposed sides, with each side quite certain about the rectitude of its own position. At first glance it would seem that abortion is an issue that is very hotly debated, but closer examination reveals that although there is indeed plenty of heat, there is no light; no debate at all.

There is no debate because both sides "argue" from different principles. And principles, once they are regarded as ultimates—like tastes—cannot be disputed. Each side can shout the inferences from its principles at the top of its lungs at the other, even knock each other on the head as if that would improve hearing, but the only ears that will hear are their own getting the echoes bouncing back to strengthen still further their own convictions. Even so, I believe there is a common ground, and that some light can be shed on the subject.

Let us be clear what our aim is; it is not to show that abortion is right or wrong—it is much more limited than that—just that each side allow freedom of conscience to the other. As no one is for imposing abortion, but some are for opposing, the argument could be considered simply one of pro-choice versus anti-choice. The crux of the matter is that some of the finest, upright people cannot in conscience allow what they see as intrinsically evil to be an option for another, even though it is right by his, or in this case, her conscience. What we seek to bring about is a state of mind in the anti-choice camp that will permit them to have free consciences in allowing others to use theirs.

To accomplish that, all that should be necessary is to introduce doubt to the minds of the anti-choice, to challenge their certitude sufficiently so as to induce them to give the benefit of that doubt to the pro-choice people. To put it another way: that even in a non-democratic society, abortion ceases to be the concern of government.

I propose to examine the Catholic principles on which the strength of its opposition to abortion is based and show how untenable it is. The Catholic position is buttressed by the dogmatic belief that a human immortal soul exists at the moment of conception. Without that base, the whole position is weakened.

Personally, I believe that it can be conclusively demonstrated that a human soul does not exist at the moment of conception, but if my presentation does little more than bring at least a reasonable doubt to the minds of all others, that should be sufficient in a somewhat theocratic society to remove the issue from the public domain and place it in the private.

I must admit that but for subjective or personal experiences, it is to be very much doubted if I would ever have departed from my own dogmatism. Had my life not been deeply affected, it is questionable that I would have reflected so long on the issue. My philosophy was aided by my gut.

I hope to show that the conclusions or applications of one position are not incompatible with the principles of the other; at the very least, that there is a middle ground that both can agree on. In doing so, I may open a window on how the process took place in me.

It would be no mean beginning if in this first part, a reasonable doubt as to the presence of human soul at the moment of conception be acknowledged by both sides. Although, I see it as conclusive, even so, doubt should be adequate to remove the issue from the public domain and place it in that of the individual conscience.

The Catholic position, which has a theological base, has been compared to the genetic. It is true that the genetic position supports the Catholic, but it also helps by its difference to highlight the Catholic position. Geneticists assert that human life is present from the moment of fertilization because the genetic codes of the parents are present. That definitely does not detract from Catholic teaching. But according to the Catholic teaching I received, God infuses a human soul at the moment of conception, and it is that affirmation which gives such strength to the church's doctrine.

The chromosomes from both parents that are united in the offspring, I am assured by scientists, are not exclusive to human beings, but common to primates, in fact, all animals and vegetables as well. The genes from these chromosome sets also determine the unique characteristics of the offspring of other animals. Scientists are now engaged in experimenting with the genetic inheritance of tomatoes. What is exclusive to the human being, according to Catholic tradition, is that an immortal soul is present from the moment of conception.

That is the teaching that has as one of its consequences the bizarre attempts to baptize well-nigh invisible fetuses that are miscarried in the early stages. The geneticist as such has no concern for the miscarried fetus, as to whether words, water, and intentions exist that would determine its fate, whether its eternity was to be Heaven or Limbo. Nor would the geneticist have to worry about the philosophical distinction between right and privilege that allows one to maintain that the soul of the unbaptized is not deprived of a right if he or she exists forever in Limbo, even if those that are baptized are privileged to enjoy the eternal bliss of heaven.

To exemplify the distinction between right and privilege: If I walk up to somebody in the street and hand him a pound, a dollar, or a million, that is something to which he is not entitled; it is not a right; he is privileged. Nobody else should complain that he is being deprived of or denied a right. Even so, that distinction has not been adequate to save many would-be parents from untold agony because of the privilege denied their offspring.

Nor would the geneticist concern himself with such hair-splitting distinctions that forbid the removal of a diseased fertilized egg, but allows a diseased part of the fallopian tube to be removed, inevitably resulting in the loss of the same fertilized egg. The desirability of the loss of the egg is acknowledged, but it must be brought about unintentionally or indirectly.

Neither do I think the geneticist would have determined that my stepmother was not to be saved at the expense of taking a fetus that the doctors decided could not be successfully delivered. Mind you, if there had been one case in history at that time—1936—of a five-month-old fetus surviving outside the womb, the theologians might have split a hair, permitted the fetus to be removed and allowed my stepmother to live. Her death left sorrowing among others, a widower, seven children, an aging father, and an invalid sister.

I think it would have been all right to pray for a miscarriage, to storm heaven; to pray for a happening that it was considered murder to do directly. There is a world of difference between genetic science and theology—the difference between life and death.

We must reflect on the theological principle from which flows Catholic practice. It is Catholic teaching that a soul is infused at the moment of conception; that it is this that sets it off from the animal kingdom and makes a split-second-old fetus more noble and valuable in its being than the most gifted animal, for example Lassie, Affirmed, Spectacular Bid, Master McGrath, or even the last pregnant female whose death would terminate a species: tigers, lions, elephants, etc. Why...even the whole animal kingdom.

It is this principle, then, that an immortal soul is present at the moment of conception, that must be our prime concern. But our first question must be, what is a soul?

The church adopted the exposition of the ancient Greek philosopher Aristotle in its definition of the soul. The soul is the form or essence of the living body. It is also its intelligibility. As form it does not differ from the principle of life of the rest of what lives—an animal is animated, has an anima, a soul.

How does the human soul differ from all other souls? What is so germane to this study is that the human soul is also a spirit. Because of matter it is an individual member of the human species. But as matter is necessary to compose a complete human, the soul is considered an impure spirit. Angels are pure spirits; no matter is involved. It is the soul as spirit that enables it to exist apart from its body. A human is composed of body and soul, matter and spirit. How do matter and spirit differ? Matter is quantified, is extended, occupies space and can be divided, theoretically, *ad infinitum.* Spirit, on the other hand, is unmagnified, is not extended, does not have parts outside parts that permit division. It is simple, so indivisible.

The soul, then, shares in the two worlds of matter and spirit. With the rest of the animal world, a human is subject to mortality and so dies. The soul then leaves the body or ceases to inform it. It is in virtue of being spirit, that the human soul alone of all the animated kingdom can exist apart from its body. But as the soul is spirit, unquantified, having no parts, there is nothing that is subject to separation; it cannot die.

The only thing conceivable to its destruction is annihilation by Divine Power, or as some might prefer, by the Divine Power ceasing to sustain. But whereas God can create, annihilate or cease to sustain, He cannot kill. The simplicity of spirit means that there is nothing in its nature that makes it subject to a separation of part from part.

It is such that an indivisible soul, we are told, is infused at the precise moment when the sperm from the male meets the egg from the female. Matter and spirit enter a strange alliance.

Now, the crucial question: As the soul is indivisible, what takes place when more than one birth results from a single fertilization? Identical twins. The one soul by definition cannot become two. Are we to say that in this case God waits until after the division has taken place before infusing the souls, or should we simply accept that a human soul is not present at the moment of conception?

Surely this consideration alone should furnish ample grounds for the most ardent Catholic fundamentalist to have an easier conscience in letting others choose differently. In practice, that abortion should not be a subject for a public referendum.

Nature's Evaluation of the Human Fetus

The conclusion just reached is of paramount importance when the mode of contraception that prevents the sperm and egg from meeting is compared with the one in which the egg is rejected shortly after fertilization. For this latter may be designated abortion, and therefore, by implication, murder, if there is a soul present. If there were no further consideration, that alone makes the conclusion we have reached worthwhile. Once the existence of the soul is discounted, murder is ruled out.

But we must go further in our evaluation of the fetus. Let us move beyond that short period of time when subdivisions will have ceased.

My medical knowledge is rather limited, so when my wife returned from the doctor after having had one of her miscarriages, and related the doctor's remark that when a woman turns the age of thirty-five there is an increasing incidence of bad eggs, which usually results in miscarriages, and that these take place usually during the first three months of pregnancy, I was given food for thought.

My wife had three miscarriages of which we were aware, all in the first three months. (Three of the four children we have, now so much part of our lives, would never have existed had these miscarriages not taken place.) One of the twins who helps me understand this marvel of human ingenuity before me, the computer, would not exist. Nor would his twin sister, who gives so much of herself to those limited in their development, and is so beloved by the recipients, be there for them.

I must confess that I had a gut reaction against baptizing

the first fetus miscarried—my wife could not look at it. It was I who discovered it on top of the toilet seat, a little sack of water, transparent, almost totally invisible to the human eye. I called up the priest to make sure that I was to perform the service of baptism. His answer was in the affirmative. He himself was not for performing the function. I reflected that in practice he was making a distinction between the fetus and an unbaptized baby in danger of death, an event which would have brought him running. Baptizing a fetus requires much more expertise and detachment.

I said the words and hoped there was no need to pour water as the fetus was immersed in it. I couldn't see it, anyway. At the second occurrence, I said words halfheartedly and somewhat ashamedly over the toilet bowl. By the time of the third incident, I started to feel that the whole thing was ridiculous and an insult to God, and I let the fetus go into the sewerage without ceremony.

It seemed totally unfitting to attribute such requirements as coming from the Supreme Perfect Being. To baptize or not to baptize became a case of, "I'll be damned if I do, and I'll be damned if I don't." Will I have to carry around with me the gnawing thought that one of my offspring will never see the face of God because of my lack of 'humility?' Or, I'll not see the face of God if I repeatedly insult Him by performing these bizarre rites. It may not be out of place to observe, in passing, that had I not been intimately involved with a number of miscarriages, I could well be a pure armchair philosopher to this day.

To continue our reflections on the frequency of miscarriages. A close relation of mine had very many, eight I think, and two successful births. It is not unreasonable to infer that in the course of history, there could well have been as many miscarriages as births, if not more. And until very recent times, many miscarriages would not have been distinguishable from monthly periods. What was the fate of those fetuses! Think of all those that dropped by the side of work fields in China, Africa, and the world over. Surely we cannot pass lightly over such occurrences without experiencing some doubt about the value of a fetus.

An acceptable mode of philosophical reasoning is that if a doctrine can be reduced to absurdity, it is refuted. It seems to me that I was doing precisely that when on walking out of a college in New Jersey and observing the huge sewerage drains opened up right across the parking lot to the buildings opposite, I remarked to the students: "Did somebody have a miscarriage!" Such would be the logic of Catholic teaching. A saint, St. Francis Xavier, I think, said, "Cross the seas, save a soul and die." So, surely drains should be torn up.

A prominent cleric objected, saying a pregnant woman should then carry around a portable commode. Not according to what I was saying, but according to the church's teaching, was my reply. But, he countered, "If one is not sure, one does not fire a shot into the wood, lest somebody be in there," implying that baptism, lest a soul is present, is backing off somewhat from the dogmatic position. But, again, precisely. If muffled sounds are heard after a cave-in and one is not sure a human being is trapped, no effort is spared until certainty is established. Many animal lovers would do as much for a cat or a dog or other animal.

One need not go on to see the absurdity to which the Catholic position is reduced, and that the church, in practice, makes little or no attempt to follow out the logic of its own teaching. Now and again we may hear of a drain being torn up to find a lost diamond ring, or mining for gold or oil, not to mention the wholesale slaughter and mass destruction in Iraq for oil, but never a digging or a search for a lost fetus.

So far we have established on biological grounds that a soul cannot be present at the moment of fertilization, and secondly, we have shown that to accept the presence of a soul at a much later date would result in absurd practices. From this we may infer that neither is a human soul present at a later date.

But before moving on, I think we should be aware that the reduction to absurdity hinges on the need for baptism and that that same absurdity could be used as an argument to show there must be no need for baptism. This could be a basis from which theologians could legitimately claim that some other method such as desire of the parents should be adequate—or that Limbo is pretty good anyway, much better than what most of us are trying to hang onto here, although this latter would sound pretty thin. However, for these reasons it would be well to consider the frequency of miscarriages from another aspect.

The church advises us to use God as our model. In the encyclical on Birth Control, *Humani Vitae,* we are told that the Divine Reason placed the infertile period in women so that the human reason could discover it and use it, a moral way of avoiding conception.

Perhaps there is also a lesson to be learned from another pattern in female reproduction. Reflect for a moment on how the Author of Nature acts with regard to the human fetus. In the course of history, miscarriages must be in the order of billions and billions. Does that give any inkling as to the value God puts on a fetus? At the very least we can infer that God is blasé about their fate. It is He that has created a built-in natural or spontaneous rejection for defective ones. And the normal pattern according to which this rejection occurs is during the first three months of pregnancy—the same period of time within which abortions are almost one hundred per cent safe, very minor affairs.

Were those defective fetuses not rejected, can we infer that the offspring would not have enjoyed worthwhile lives? Does it not seem reasonable, then, to suggest that abortions within that time span are imitations of nature, a miscarriage being but a natural abortion?

To equate, as has been done, the number of abortions that took place in the United States in one year with the deaths in the Nazi concentration camps is to imply that God is a Being of whom Hitler was only a pale reflection. I must confess to having said something similar to that in a public address in New York some thirty years ago, and understandably caused a Jewish lady to explode in anger.

We are led to infer, then, both from the practice of the Catholic church with its attitude to the discharged fetus, and the practice of the Author of Nature with its prodigality in rejecting fetuses, that, unless we want to insult both human and Divine reason, up to the first three months of its gestation, the fetus should not be granted the dignity of human personhood, and therefore, should not be protected by law.

Whether or not the fetus develops to become a human being should rest in the same domain in which it resided before fertilization occurred, in the private and not in the public. At the very least there are ample grounds for the anti-choice fundamentalist to convert to an easier conscience in allowing others the exercise of theirs.

Abortion and the Might Have Been

Although the need to consider the young fetus as a human being has been discounted, it is necessary, nevertheless, to consider it as a "might have been" human being. Had the young fetus not developed to be me, this person would never be. And it is this thought of "the might have been" that remains to plague many, if that "might have been" did not materialize as a result of an abortion or a miscarriage. I wonder would he by now be a six-foot-plus blond, blue-eyed male or a petite brunette?, etc.

In one way or another we have been conditioned to think of the "might have been" in relation to a miscarriage or an abortion when the union of egg and sperm had taken place, but "the might have beens" which were no less definite, that did not take place because the egg and sperm did not meet causes no concern. There is little regret for the "might have been" that did not result because sexual relations did not take place at all, although a very definite unique combination of chromosomes would have resulted. Indeed this latter is usually an occasion for rejoicing.

For many people that is because of the belief that the Hand of God was not forced to issue a soul concomitant to an illicit union. I contend that there is no material difference between the "might have been" due to sexual relations that did not take place, and the "might have been" due to an abortion or miscarriage, once the infusion of a soul is discounted.

Each time a conception occurs, it is by a definite two at a definite time. A different couple pairing at the same time or the same couple at a different time would have led to a different combination and a different potential person or persons. Were it otherwise, there could not even be siblings.

Some people know exactly when they conceive. One friend told me the morning after the night before on each of the two times she became pregnant. Another person knew in the case of three pregnancies.

Equally well could it be maintained that a very definite, particular human being did not result from that mid-summer night bonfire revel in Ballinrea, when a certain individual purposely lagged behind on the road home by repeatedly knocking the chain off his bike to prevent his catching up with the beautiful girl ahead who was waiting for him. The offspring would be about fifty by now.

Because of such restraint by very many people, countless definite particulars will never see the light.

I have tried desperately, and with the blessing of the church, to prevent acts which resulted in births. Perhaps in some I was successful, in others it was much regretted that I failed, and offspring resulted. I recall two that were born in Scotland, whose conceptions I failed to prevent. In one instance the couple, under my bidding, did leave the hostel, but came back later and managed to smuggle out the mattress to an outside shed. The offspring of my failures would now be over fifty and very possibly parents, even grandparents themselves, by this time, progenitors of others that would not exist either if I had been successful.

Then there was a very particular case in which a powerful man of some fame was pounding on the other side of a locked door from me in the Globe Hotel in Dublin. My success was only temporary. Ultimately, there, too, I was a failure. Offspring resulted, although, most likely a different offspring than had I not interfered. Because of the pedigree, I believe, the infant was adopted into rather high English society. I still feel sorry that the famous father never learned of his paternity—his ex-wife married Marlon Brando. Perhaps the offspring is a Tory M.P. about as old as John Majors.

Much more recently I was a failure in preventing illicit unions that led to births. In some cases, I know the results of my failures—delightful children. Of course, I did not see the results of my successes. I've just seen on TV in support of the anti-choice position, a parade of individuals that would not have existed had not the anti-choice people prevailed. But I can assure the reader that there are quite a few people in a few different countries that could point the finger at me and say, "If you had had your way—the church's way—I would not exist."

I could go on and on, and perhaps to convince many I should, but, briefly, what I am saying is that in terms of potentiality or the "might have been," to prevent or deny intercourse at certain times just as definitely prevents a definite conception, a definite union of a genetic code and a definite person being born, as does a miscarriage or an abortion. And although at times individuals may wonder and possibly regret, too, not having had the illicit union, the church is glad and rejoices that such a sex act did not occur, and by implication, the consequent "might have been" that never will be. Such is true even in the case of bishop or pope.

Not too long ago, a student in my class who I found exceptionally attractive, spoke with me on the phone. What she said had got right by me before I realized what was said, "I, and I'm sure many girls in the class, would love to have a baby by you." I'm sorry, I could have had a parade on TV all on my own. But there is none to condemn me. Definitely not the non-births.

I am sorry if I seem to belabor this point, but all evidence is to show how difficult many people, brought up with a certain background, find it to see the simple implication of what I am saying. Time and time again I meet with the difficulty experienced over the possible births. Obviously, long and hard reflection is necessary.

Some time ago, since beginning this study in fact, I met a

young bride who was crushed as a result of a miscarriage some time before. When I remarked to her that but for miscarriages, three of my children would not exist, she at first did not comprehend my meaning, and then when understanding came to her, she blurted out, "In all my long weeks of depression, no one ever said that to me." And I added: "Think of the one you did not have because you did not marry or sexually relate at an earlier date." She did conceive again and bore a child that would never be but for the miscarriage.

From the standpoint of a definite genetic code and a unique individual, it is immaterial whether in terms of "the might have been" we prevent the conception—be that by abstention or otherwise—or the birth. Once our evaluation is based on the existence of a soul, we are forced to have a totally different perspective. It is the belief in the existence of a soul at conception that makes sense of the practice or rather—the practice being very weak—the teaching of the Catholic church.

Whereas the church is glad that certain sex acts and consequent "might have beens" did not take place, on the other hand, once the conception has taken place, it turns its full battery of guns the other way to insure the births take place as well, even to giving it priority over the mother's life. But to repeat *ad nauseam,* in terms of what the actual result would be, a particular individual or individuals, there is no difference before or after the sex act.

Perhaps it deserves more than a passing reference to observe that the church, having failed to prevent an illicit union, and then being adamant that the birth takes place, has traditionally transferred the illicitness of the union to the offspring so he or she bore the shame of illegitimacy. Many things were denied the bastard.

If allowed to become a priest, he was definitely not allowed to become a bishop. I knew one lovely lady it prevented from becoming a nun; she remained a sort of lay nun. The distinction between right and privilege is used here, too. Nobody has a right to the privileges to which the illegitimate are denied access. It is a nice distinction. All are created equal, but some are privileged.

To rule is one of those privileges. Some readers may remember from history that the Pope declared Queen Elizabeth I of England's subjects exempt from their allegiance on the grounds that Elizabeth was illegitimate. This distinction continues with the British crown. Although William IV had ten children, all illegitimate, by the Irish actress Dorothea Jordan, it was Victoria, the daughter of a younger brother, who inherited the throne. A thousand years ago the illegitimates fared better. Harold was the illegitimate son of Canute, and William the Conqueror conquered England with the Pope's blessing.

But the strangest quirk of history must be the Pope repudiating Elizabeth I on the grounds of illegitimacy, when it was such a short time before that a pope of illegitimate birth, Pope Clement VII, ruled the church when the queen's father broke from Rome. It's a wonder Henry didn't think of that one to justify his break in order to marry the queen's mother, Anne Boleyn.

However, let's not think that out-of-wedlock births are not acceptable. Royal bastards are ennobled with the prefix "Fitz." An illegitimate son of William IV was called FitzClarence when his father was the Duke of Clarence, and so on. Even James II, he of the Boyne, fathered FitzJames, the First Duke of Berwick, with the cooperation of Arrabella Churchill, sister of the First Duke of Marlborough, the same who took Kinsale and Cork in his support of William of Orange. Imagine if FitzJames had been able to inherit the throne. After the Boyne, he married the widow of Patrick Sarsfield.

We can make all the distinctions we like with right and privilege. The simple reality is that the sting of illegitimacy is still very much part of our inheritance. So, many of those that insist on the birth, insist on one being born with one stroke against him or her. Even royalty is not excluded. Only just recently the children of Caroline of Monaco were elevated to legitimacy by the Vatican, and thus enabled to inherit the throne. The union from which they were born had not been recognized by the church. So, although royalty is not excluded, perhaps it does provide the edge in having the stigma of illegitimacy removed.

In considering the "might have been" we may like to contemplate how poorer or richer the world could have been without some of its famous or infamous bastards. Do we consider the already mentioned William the Conqueror, *cognomen Bastardus?* And was not the learned Erasmus, Prince of the Humanists, the offspring of a priest and a serving girl? Leonardo da Vinci, one of the great geniuses of all time, resulted from the illicit union of a prominent lawyer and a lower class woman. Boccaccio, who wrote *Decameron,* reputed one of the most famous books in all literature, was born out of wedlock to a French mother and an Italian father, and, of course, as is more generally known, the ruthless Cesare Borgia was the son of Pope Alexander VI.

Which way do we want to view all those births? It could be maintained that but for the pro-life forces, for Catholic teaching, they never would have been born. And neither would all those descended from them, including every English monarch from 1066 up to the present queen and on to Prince Charles and his children. There might have been no Norman Conquest of England, and no Henry II to send Strongbow to Ireland, no Magna Carta, and no Henry VIII to break from Rome, and no James I to promote the Plantation of Ulster, and no James II to be opposed by William III (his nephew/son-in-law who, of course, wouldn't have existed either) at the Boyne, and—no Six-

County problem today and its current cease-fire. And on the wider map, no Wilhelm II to push out Bismarck and encourage World War I, or Nicholas II of Russia to provoke the 1917 revolution, setting the stage for world communism and, of course, no World War II, cold war, Korea, or Vietnam—and my friends could still be alive today.

On the other hand, if the church's teaching had been observed, all those genetic inheritances would never have seen the darkness of the womb in the first place. Would the world have been a better place? The answer to that we will never know. It would definitely be a different world. That any of us is here is a much lesser chance than winning the lottery, but somebody does win.

Considering the "might have been" is a total exercise in futility. What is, is. "Many a rose is born to blush unseen." And not only in the "Country Church Yard" but also in the world of genetic possibility there is a "mute inglorious Milton, a Cromwell guiltless of his country's blood," a Jack the Ripper, or a Hitler, or an Einstein. And many a plain, John Doe.

One clear-cut and important distinction must be observed between the opposing camps of pro- and anti-choice. For the most part, both sides accept the freedom to become pregnant as a right in the individual, but once the pregnancy has taken place, the great divide appears. One side sees itself as duty bound to compel all pregnant individuals to develop and nourish the life that is within it and bring it to birth, for some, even at the cost of the mother's own life. For this group, as soon as the pregnancy has occurred, the issue has immediately been removed from the private, even out of the family, to the public domain. The impregnated woman has no more say in the matter than all other people the world over.

The other side is certain that the same freedom that existed to become pregnant also exists toward giving birth. If the person were not able to give a new human being a chance for a full life, then, according to her judgment, it would be wrong to give birth. In conscience, for the latter an unwanted pregnancy remains an unwanted birth. For the other side, a vehemently unwanted pregnancy becomes as vehemently a wanted birth, not just for themselves, but for everybody else as well. The concern of one side is life leading to birth; the other maintains that to justify the birth there must be life after birth. For the former, the world at large has a duty to defend the right of the second old fetus to exist. Its guarantee to the good life once born is none of their business.

It has been demonstrated that birth can be related to desirability of offspring without the mediation of abstract principles, which do not hold up to scrutiny, and that if it is accepted that wanted births and not unwanted pregnancies are the only justification for taking on the responsibility of bringing a new human being into the world, there would rarely be a call for an abortion in the case of an advanced pregnancy, unless something such as danger to the mother's life becomes an issue.

Little reflection is needed to realize what ease of mind the above considerations will bring to parents and others responsible for teenagers, and all those not ready for parenthood. I am not entering into a discussion as to how extramarital sex should be viewed, but simply stating that the fear and apprehension of unwanted pregnancies, whether within or without marriage, can be greatly reduced if people are thoroughly convinced that an unwanted pregnancy can remain an unwanted birth.

It is one and the same genetic inheritance that does not develop. So, with an easy conscience, what was an unwanted birth the night before, can remain an unwanted birth the morning after.

We can now return to our stated purpose, introducing

sufficient doubt in the minds of those against choice so as to permit them in conscience to allow conscience to be the guide of others in the matter of abortion. Our exposition, by showing the weakness in the pro-life position, should do more than introduce doubt, but we will settle for doubt. Doubt is sufficient to remove the issue of abortion altogether from the public sector, and rest it in the individual conscience. Abortion ceases to be a subject for a referendum.

Abortion and Democracy

So far we confined ourselves to one single issue, abortion and whose right it is to choose. To induce all to grant freedom of conscience to everyone else, we examined what we understand to be the principles on which the pro-life, anti-choice partisans base their conscientious objection, and demonstrated that those principles fall far short of what should be demanded by the pro-life, anti-choice advocates.

The debate on abortion should now be closed. But suppose it were still open because some are still unconvinced, or a further issue, similarly dogmatic, surfaces? Is there any principle of at least toleration that will have people agree to differ? Can each of us in conscience go his own way without feeling it incumbent on us to insist that those that differ conform to our view? Or, if we feel that we must bring pressure to bear on others, can we distinguish between using moral and legal force?

A threefold distinction is being introduced: a difference that we can accept in each other without interference; a difference in which we feel obligated to use moral pressure, but not legal, and a difference that is of such a nature that we judge that the legal power of the state should be enlisted to enforce our position. Of course, it is the second and third that are pertinent to our discussion.

Is there any principle whereby a *modus vivendi* or coexistence can prevail between diametrically opposed values, so that we readily accept that we will not seek the strong arm of the state to enforce our certitude, but we will confine ourselves to moral pressure?

In our approach up to now, we sought to diffuse the contention by showing that there were not enough grounds for dogmatism, making it manifest that judgment should be for the private conscience. We then inferred that, of course, it should not be subject to state authority. But further reflection reveals that neither should abortion be part of Catholic dogmatism. Was it not Catholic principles we used to expose the weakness in the church's position? But even if the church's position were not refuted, their teaching is still no function of state.

So our task now is much more formidable, to distinguish between what may of its nature be considered a legitimate area of state involvement, and one that irrespective of the seriousness and/or truth of the matter, does not fall within state jurisdiction. Is there a principle to guide us, in virtue of which, even though we are absolutely certain, with no doubt in our minds about values, we will still adamantly maintain that it is no business of the state; that it is for the individual conscience alone to decide?

We believe there is such a principle, and that abortion comes under that heading. As a result of further exposition, we hope the readers, though still having little or no doubt that abortion is wrong, will nevertheless adopt a philosophy that makes state interference wrong also.

The reader may suspect that had we embraced such an approach at the outset, the foregoing chapters need not have been written at all. The answer, of course, is yes. But to convince against ingrained tradition is not easy. Unfortunately, principles that are used to support an existing way of life (even slavery), rather than as a guide to living, are much more readily embraced when they justify existing practices than when they oppose. Actually our purpose is to induce a state of mind that is comfortable with not using the state to enforce values that arise out of religious beliefs, or all values considered fundamental. In truth our aim is to move people towards democracy.

Concern and the effort to change the values of others will prevail. The difference, the huge difference, is a willingness not to use the state in its endeavor. The pulpit and all other means of communication may be used for the purposes of moral persuasion. The state alone is excepted. To except the state, we must know the nature or proper function of the state. Our approach, then, is to examine the nature of the state so we can explicate the proper relationship between government and the individual.

Up to the present we have been arguing within the framework of theological principles. We now reason from the democratic. In the former, authority is from the top down, and conscience is formed by it. In the latter, authority is from the bottom up and that authority is subject to the individual conscience. Again, the former is not, by its very nature, disposed to tolerate the conscience that differs from it. Execution has often been the lot of the conscientious objector.

As in the early part of our study, we had to treat the nature of the soul, or the essence of a human being, so we must now study the nature of the state that purports to be the controlling agency, not only with abortion, but with many other issues of a fundamental nature. As our state is alleged to be a democratic one, a study of the nature of democracy is primary.

A little reflection will convince the reader that he is not too clear in his own mind as to what democracy is. Perhaps even less clear than he was about the nature of the soul. My questioning of a number of people revealed little more than a not-too-clear reference to majority rule. Of course the obvious question is, majority about what and majority of what?

In this short compass and against the bulwark of tradition, to explain democracy is somewhat formidable. To move the anti-choice conscience on abortion toward accepting choice is no easy undertaking. To have democracy espoused, a philosophy accepted that would extend choice without state entanglement to a much wider range of human values, constitutes a challenge of mammoth proportions.

What are the basic elements of democracy?

According to democratic theory, we are all members of the human race; we form one community with the rest of mankind the moment we are born. As such, we are subject to one universal law. Which law is based on the nature of man, and is anterior to government?

From our membership in the human race arises rights and duties to one another. The rights and duties that arise out of that broad-based and essential relationship of human brotherhood cannot be abrogated or foresworn. Being born is the only qualification for membership. Second, without abrogating that membership with its rights and duties that we are born into, there can be other memberships *voluntarily* entered into or accepted for mutual advantages, such as to protect one's rights, or what belongs to one. Membership in the voluntary communities also establishes rights and duties. These voluntary communities are communities within the larger universal human community to which we do not and cannot cease to belong. Human values must always prevail.

The first voluntary community for humans is the family. Although voluntary, it is necessary for the survival of the human race, but so strong is the instinctual drive to sexual union and procreation, that families have, without outside pressure, spontaneously formed. The community of man, the human race, is composed of families. Nothing more than birth grants membership to both communities.

The rights and duties arising out of membership in the human race are based on the nature of man. They are anterior to government. Government results from the particular membership voluntarily entered into in common with others.

Theoretically, the state originated as a result of some members of the universal brotherhood of man agreeing to associate for their common defense and benefit. Government was limited in its involvement with its individual members by the common benefit that is the basis for the association.

The articles of association determine the extent of interference. Obligations and rights consequent to being members of the human race are not abrogated by the particular and limited relationships that exist due to state membership. But, neither is it the business of the state to enforce universal rights and duties, for that is not its purpose. What the state can enforce are the dues for common benefit. It is our duty to contribute to the implementation of justice, police protection, public roads, etc.

The state does not exist to enforce the universal moral law either within or beyond its boundaries or jurisdiction. But the individual not having his membership in the human race curtailed or abrogated by state membership is still open to enjoy human rights and exercise human duties in the free exercise of his conscience, which include helping and defending a brother in need, both within and beyond the state boundaries.

The individual's conscience is exclusively his guide in his interactions with the rest of the human race. Conceivably, he may find it necessary to join with others to enable him to enjoy its free exercise, but no one would separate from the human race to have freedom of conscience, least of all freedom of conscience within the family, curtailed.

As conscience is the very essence of what it is to be human, should conscience need protection, what better, though limited, association than the state to oppose the foe?

The nature of a real democratic community or state may be more easily understood if an analogy is made between state membership and membership in a private club. Suppose a group of people decide to form a vacation club because of the mutual advantages it brings to its members. The constitution and bylaws are concerned with nothing other than vacations. It has no business interfering with anything but vacations. For instance, the individual member's private life must be immaterial to it.

Members may decide on moral or other grounds not to have any more association with other members than club membership specifies, but that it must do as private individuals, being members of the human race.

In no way can the authority of the club be invoked to bring pressure of any sort to bear on the individual member or members in matters not related to vacations. Although as members of the human race, we may feel justified in shunning, ostracizing, boycotting, or even killing them.

I am asserting that much is being imposed by states that arises out of membership in the human race, and therefore, the concern of all mankind is not within the lawful jurisdiction of the state. The question, then, becomes not one of good and evil, but the propriety of state involvement in what is regarded as a universal value.

A new dimension is added if some within the state do not share the same values that the controlling members or majority seeks to impose on them. Let's keep the comparison with a vacation club in mind. It is as individual members of the human race, and not as club members, that they should unite in trying to right the human wrong. Democratically, Irishmen, Americans, members of all states and no state, as human beings could have volunteered for Tiananmen Square or Yugoslavia.

We may query what it is, or rather, how the state, by democratic definition the protector of individual conscience, has become the enemy. It would be naive to think that there ever was a state formed according to the contractual theory, that people agreed mutually to come together for definite and specific purposes. Ironically, but logically, the state is the one community not founded according to the contractual theory. Were political units so established, the democratic challenge would never have arisen. But communities, tribes, states, and empires existed long before such writers as John Locke and John Jacques Rousseau countered and challenged with democratic philosophy.

Still, the principle of contract or agreement is valid. The true litmus test should be the answer to the simple question: Is this a community, all things being equal, which everyone would freely join, or in which they would want to continue membership? The weakness in the test is, there is no such community. But obviously no one would freely join a community at the price of being deprived of the free exercise of conscience, no more than a person would join a community that would result in enslavement. Although there may be no real choice if all states are slave states or no state allows freedom of conscience.

Obstacles to Democracy

I believe we can pinpoint the three basic elements in the nonfulfillment of democracy. One is the tradition of the union of church and state, when divine right monarchs and church leaders saw it as their legitimate right, even duty, to burn heretics—those with nonconforming consciences—at the stake.

Second, the almost immediate perversion of democracy with the assumption that nation-states were sovereign and humanity was not.

Third, then confusing democracy with universal suffrage and equating majority rule with its fulfillment.

Democratic theory with its notion of contract and ownership is much closer to the beginnings of political units than what eventually became kingdoms and empires by divine right, and far distant from the latter-day sovereign nation-states.

The predatory aspect of our human nature was largely ignored by Locke. Locke concentrated on replacing the monarch. He envisioned the contract as between people and monarch, and saw no danger from the people, of one member oppressing another. Rousseau was quite an improvement. He made the distinction between the people as governed and the people as sovereign, and was well aware that one member might want to suppress the rest, but it took Mill to really sound the alarm, and coin the phrase, "the tyranny of the majority."

The majority slipped unobtrusively into assuming the role of the divine right kings, only much worse when wedded to the concept of sovereign nation-states. The sovereignty of the majority replaced the sovereignty of the king.

And, as in earlier times, after the violent overthrow of a government, the religion of the new became the established one, with the government coming to power seeking to use its office to impose its morality on all. Such governments are convinced that they are justified in doing so. They have a mandate. Because elected, they claim the mantle of democracy.

But it is not the mode of appointment to office that is essentially democratic, but the limit and source of power exercised. Kings and popes of old had to be proclaimed by the people, but once elected, they had powers in excess of the powers of the people. They were endowed from on high with a measure of divinity. The people were henceforth obeying not themselves, but God.

Currently there is an expression in the English language, the "moral majority." John Stewart Mill astutely made a distinction between morality and law, observing that in England, though the burden of law was light, that of morality was heavy. In the land of liberty his worst nightmare is straining at the bit, the union of law and morality, the subversion of democracy in the name of democracy, the wolf in sheep's clothing. The tyranny of the majority threatens to become the tyranny of the moral majority.

Should the moral majority succeed, whence, then, redress or escape! The old tyrannies were overthrown when there was enough strength to do so. The question is: how to overthrow a moral majority that will use the state to impose its morals on all, that will claim a mandate from the people, a "democratic" election as the source of their authority? (And what if the moral majority is ousted? If the principle of moral imposition by a majority is accepted, what's to prevent the new "immoral" minority being coerced in turn?)

In the nondemocratic systems, authority was from the top down, from God and through the king or government. An individual conscience would not be tolerated did it differ from absolute authority. According to democracy, authority is from the bottom up; the government can have no power which it does not get from the individual, and that power is very limited indeed.

The moral majority lays claim to an authority from the bottom up, but it seeks to impose standards from on high, standards that the majority considers universal. We have reverted to the old system; the human election transformed by divine ordination, the majority assuming the role of divine right kings. Such a hybrid of democracy and theocracy can prove to be the greatest of all tyrannies. As I said before, how escape? Whence freedom?

To reiterate, the universal moral law is anterior to government and no business of it. The jurisdiction of a democratic state is limited to this world's activities, and then only to those delegated by its members for the common good. In these limited areas a majority may determine the best course of action within the agreed extent of state involvement. That majority may be simple, two-thirds or four-fifths, according to the gravity of the subject matter. In some cases unanimity may be demanded.

But no majority can determine the morality of anything. We know that a majority of all minus one will not make abortion right for that one. She rightfully will still go by her own conscience. Morality cannot be democratically legislated. If morality is legislated, the system is not democratic; legislated morality and democracy is a contradiction in terms.

As the legislation of morality and democracy are mutually exclusive, with a moral majority, democracy ceases. If the nature of democracy is not understood, that may seem a very strong affirmation, but if confirmation is necessary, we need look no further than the statement by Cardinal Joseph Bernardin of Chicago. Speaking for the Catholic bishops in October 1985, in which he left no doubt that Catholics who personally support the church's position on abortion, but concede others the right to dissent against it, are also violating God's law, an unequivocal statement that Catholicism and democracy are mutually exclusive.

They are exclusive not because one side affirms a universal moral law and the other does not, but because one side insists that their version must be imposed on all. "The church's teaching on this matter is binding, not only because the church says so, but because this teaching expresses the objective demands placed on all of us by the inherent dignity of human life."

It is not just a discipline of the church, like fasting or holidays of obligation, binding just on Catholics. It is a universal value binding on all, and as such, an individual dissenting conscience must not be permitted. This example of the fundamentalist mind is no less than that experienced in other fundamentalist states. If the reader thought democracy the answer to many of the world's ills, he must learn that we are beating against impervious walls, and why it was necessary for me at the outset to show that abortion is not against Catholic principles, because the fetus should not be accorded the "inherent dignity of human life."

My argument was threefold: the impossibility of the subdivision of the spiritual soul in the case of multiple births from a single fertilization; the example of God's nature in the billions of natural abortions, or miscarriages; and the absurd practices to which granting the fetus "the inherent dignity of human life" would lead.

Irish and U.S. Democracy

A closer look at Ireland and the U.S. will reveal how far short of true democracy they both fall. In Ireland a thin veneer of democracy overlies the old autocratic system. Even in the parliamentary system the party whip allows little room for the individual conscience. Ironically, nothing reveals the undemocratic nature of the state more than that odd occasion when the party whip is removed to permit its members to enjoy a free vote of conscience.

Let's take one instance, the free vote of conscience on the use of contraceptives by the constituents. It was not the constituents who voted—which would still not make it democratic, but the tyranny of the majority—It was the Dáil members. The country witnessed the spectacle of the then Taoiseach who introduced the bill and one of his cabinet ministers cross the aisle to vote against easy access to contraceptives.

Of course, the big question is: On what principle, philosophical, theological or otherwise, do the members of the Dáil have a free vote of conscience to determine if I am to be free to use mine? The "democratic" country did not question the procedure. Although for all I know some other individuals may have queried it as I did, by means of the "free" press and not seen their letter in print either.

In democratic terms, the government is *ultra vires* as would be the vacation club if it ordered me to send my children to a specific school. But we accept its involvement without question. We think we are democratic, but our mind-set is theocratic.

Expelling Senator Hannifin from Fianna Fail, the major

party in government, has a special twist to it. It is in microcosm an example of the dilemma facing all democrats vis-à-vis giving freedom to fundamentalists. Senator Hannifin was expelled from Fianna Fail as a result of following his conscience. The Fianna Fail party seeks to deny freedom of conscience to one member. The senator in conscience would deny freedom of conscience to the whole state. A general nondemocratic mess all round. To paraphrase John Stuart Mill, all are for freedom of conscience for their own consciences, but few for granting it to others. Few are for freedom of conscience as such.

It is easy to understand Ireland's lack of democracy. In fact, it has moved a long way toward granting freedoms. Although mimicking greatly the British parliamentary system, Ireland moved away from the establishment of a religion which is still part of the British system—so much so in fact, that the queen is head of the Church of England—although her son Charles is threatening to decline the honor while the British parliament debates the ordination of married women in the established church.

But in Ireland, where the Catholic church is almost overpoweringly influential on many of the legislators and voters, the yoke of morality is still very heavy. The church does not hesitate to use the secular law to impose its teaching. Freedom of conscience has the full protection of the law if the conscience is formed or informed by the church.

Our consideration has been concentrating on the use of government to forbid freedom of conscience. For example, in Ireland it is the use of contraceptives that was voted on, and the right to abortion. The opposition was not seeking to impose anything on anybody, just to be allowed to act according to their individual consciences. But in the U.S., there are also areas in which a departure from democratic principles is advocated.

For the sake of clarity of presentation, I am forced to use

labels such as conservative and liberal, right and left, fundamentalist and democrat. Why I say democracy is the contrary of fundamentalism is simply because fundamentalists consider it a function of government, its main function, to impose on all members a morality dictated by next-life considerations. For the democrat, it is no business at all of government. He or she is strictly neutral on moral issues. If the government has one function on the subject of morality, it is to protect all individuals in the free exercise of conscience so as not to be imposed upon or hindered by others.

Both right and left (for the student of logic) are contrary to each other. Democracy proves to be the contradiction of both, although not equidistant. The reader will be the judge. Let's take two current examples in the U.S., both relating to abortion, one of which is the legitimate area of government defending democratic freedoms, and the other which should not be the business of government at all.

The democratic aberration takes a different turn than Ireland's. In the U.S., neither liberals nor conservatives are exempt. On abortion they seem to be on totally opposite sides, and, except for their fuzzy thinking on free speech, they are. Both sides are at fault in their using the state to support their relative positions.

Let's bear in mind that it is not simply pro- and anti-choice that are in contention, but using the state to support or facilitate a position. The right wing would use the government to coerce, to forbid choice; the left to facilitate it. Both come up short on democracy.

No one is for compelling abortion, but the conservative seeks to compel birth. He is not content with being allowed the fullest freedom to communicate his views, to persuade through the pulpit and all other media, but wants to enlist the government to enforce by law his conscientious views against the consciences of others, even so far as to declare abortion murder, and by implication, a miscarriage resulting from neglect, manslaughter, the wolf of fundamentalism in the sheep's clothing of majority rule.

The liberals, for their part, seek to use the state to fund abortions. Government funding is one of the more sensitive areas in human relations. That, too, is a carryover from the days when absolute government was the norm. Obey the king, and as Louis XIV was advised by the doctors of the Sorbonne, all the wealth of the kingdom was his to use according to his will.

Income tax at all, from earlier times was considered robbery. Who does not know that, "No taxation without representation," was the cry of the American Revolution? Not long after, taxation was again the root of Shay's Rebellion. It still determines the outcome of many an election.

Gradually, the logic of the people being the source of government developed to the recognition that as government is to protect property, the only grounds for taxation, compulsory acquisition of the individual's property, must come under one of two headings, common duty or common benefit.

But to establish the particular application of such subprinciples of democracy is open to a very wide challenge. Obviously, unanimity, no matter how ideal, will not be attained, but failing that, the criterion that none is by law excluded from the benefits of taxation must be maintained. We show our appreciation of those facets of democracy by such practices as separate voting on school budgets and putting bond issues on the ballot paper. Majorities decide; but none can be excluded from the application of the benefits.

It is on the basic democratic principle, freedom of conscience, that we flounder on the rock of taxation. Compelling people to support with their taxes what is against their conscience is a carryover from authoritarian days, far removed from democracy.

Democracy, as we have clearly established already, affirms a neutral position, neither to hinder or assist where conscience is in conflict, neither to use the public purse to deny or restrict freedom of choice to one side, or assist the other.

Let's take a case in point. Only a minority and not a very large minority, at that, voted against the bill in the Senate giving approval to financing abortions for women who have been victims of rape or incest, and to women whose lives are threatened by their pregnancies. But even such a restricted measure carried by a large plurality 80–15 had fifteen percent against it. If that vote is a fair representation of the country at large, millions of people are being coerced to support with their taxes what they abhor. If there was just one constituent in opposition, to force him to support a measure that is against his conscience would be an example of the tyranny of the majority.

Is there a way out of an impasse, providing for the poor in such an important issue that would allow them the same option that has the protection by law for the rich? Why the rich and poor should have the same option in this particular issue and not other issues, such as third level education or a new suit every year, requires its own explanation. At this point in our discussion, I would suggest that the right accrues to the fetus rather than the would-not-be parents. The ideal solution would be to fund abortions from voluntary contributions. This could be done privately, but not efficiently, and the right of choice could be severely curtailed. However, the means and the practice is already at hand. Our income tax returns allow for such voluntary contributions from our taxes, and in much less sensitive areas that do not involve conscience at all.

Such a method would conform to democratic principles; it would widen the field of choice by facilitating those who want to contribute and allow freedom to those who, from poverty, could not exercise their choice, without, at the same time, compelling a single person to contribute against his or her conscience.

To protect people by law from having to contribute against their consciences is of the very essence of democracy. Unfortunately, some of those selfsame people, who would be protected from contributing against their consciences, will by their actions force doctors, who within the democratic law facilitate choice, to wear bulletproof vests and have bodyguards because they live in fear of their lives. Already doctors and bodyguards have been murdered. Then democrats must take all the means necessary to render protection against such outlaws from the democratic system, to keep fundamentalism in all its forms at bay.

How unfortunate it is that human nature is such that people will impose when they can and cry foul when imposed upon, sometimes even when forbidden to impose. Of a surety eternal vigilance is the price of liberty. The old authoritarian system is straining to take over again and under the guise of democracy. If we existed in a full democracy, our government would not have to involve itself with the freedom to choose on moral issues, but could use its energies for its appointed purpose, confining itself to what is economical and political.

Freedom of Speech and Freedom of Living

Does democracy, then, with its limitations, frustrate those who strongly want to influence the morals of others? Actually it expands their field, while testing the sincerity of their commitment. Because, although democracy forbids the use of government to impose morals within a particular community, and *a fortiori* on members of other communities, in its affirmation of membership in the human race it encourages universal concern and involvement in what each holds to be a fundamental human value.

Let's for example, again take the issue of abortion. The individuals who consider abortion a great evil, should act as missionaries worldwide, in China, India, Africa, etc. But the means used on a universal basis and in their own country are one and the same, moral not legal persuasion. We are aware that moral persuasion means full freedom to promulgate values with all the media available.

Legal persuasion carries with it the power to physically, violently, impose or oppose. This distinction is of the utmost importance in making a judgment between freedom of speech or promulgation of values or ideas, and freedom to intimidate. Confusion or lack of clarity as to the implications of democracy is much in evidence when at times freedom of speech seems to conflict with freedom of action. The issue has surfaced again on whether demonstrations against abortion as an exercise of free speech, overstep the line of demarcation so as to limit freedom of action.

I myself spoke against abortion from a stand in New York City. I often addressed gatherings in Times Square and Greenwich Village. Some did not like what I said; on occasion expressed their anger and moved on. Unfortunately, offending people is inseparable from the right of free speech. But people were free to move on. Perhaps, it would be preferable if passersby were not compelled to overhear in the first place. When I addressed crowds on London's Tower Hill and at Speaker's Corner in Hyde Park, no compulsion was involved; only those who want to hear go there. There is maximum freedom of speech without the slightest impingement on those not desiring to hear.

The line between the rights of one to speak and the right of others not to be captive audiences is perfectly balanced in London, capital of the country from which we wrested liberty. Where such a facility is not available, some judgment to strike a balance is necessary. Now, if we keep in mind what is to be achieved, the balance that will reconcile two freedoms, both part of our democratic system, freedom to express and freedom of action with no coercion, it will not require a Solomon to decide if the area chosen for demonstration, for free speech, is precisely so it can have some effect on the practitioners, make life more difficult for them to practice within the law, than if some other venue were chosen.

It is not just a question of doctor's privacy versus free speech, as has been headlined in the newspapers. It is much more speech in a location that is intended to make difficult freedom of action. Freedom of speech has an extensive area in which it can be exercised. The governing bodies go beyond what could reasonably be expected of them by inconveniencing many, so far even as to facilitate the speakers' efforts to have a very large audience, by cordoning off heavily trafficked streets at public expense and inconvenience. That is even more than the right to free speech could demand. To permit free speech, even facilitate it at public expense and inconvenience could in itself be open to challenge. But as it is available to all without exception, there is little ground for complaint except from those inconvenienced at the time.

However, there is a vast difference between publicly expounding and private targeting. Should free speech permit Nazi, anti-Semitic views, it should not be permitted outside a Jewish house of worship or the private home of a Jewish person. That would be to use intimidation, a departure from the neutral ground of democracy. Regrettably, we don't have a democratic mind-set, so much time and money is used in litigation.

It should be clear to a democrat that to picket a private residence is to selectively seek out a specific area so as to subject to pressure specific people, to deter them or force them in the direction which the picketer desires. It may not be pressure of the same order that the government applies, but it is pressure nonetheless, and the government must forbid it. The law must be used to protect the one picketed, especially one who is on the side of the law. So, picketing of such a nature is to be outlawed.

On the issue of abortion, freedom of action cannot be inhibited, while at the same time freedom of speech must be protected. The world is a very large place; all of it is open to free speech with the exception of that very limited area within which those of a different position may feel inhibited or restricted, or lose their privacy.

People are not free if they feel intimidated. And the people involved are the best judge of that; they would not go to court if they did not experience stress. So, in that vast area in which views can be freely expressed, only those areas in which even a suggestion of intimidation exists are excluded. (If it's not intended to be intimidation, why be adamant about that particular spot? Clearly the one and only consideration in choosing that exact location is its calculated effect on the actions of those who reside or practice there.) In using a neutral area for demonstration, the democratic freedom of conscience is exercised by both sides. One is free to speak *urbi et orbi;* the other enjoys freedom of action.

But the obverse side of state noninvolvement in morals within the community is that neither can it inhibit its members from exercising their universal brotherhood without. To use the above example, U.S. citizens should be free to travel the world. Most often, so-called democratic states seem to err in both directions: imposing within where it ought not, and forbidding without where it should permit, in democratic terms, ignore.

Were all the energy used in attempting to forbid parents the freedom to give or not give birth—denying them the responsibility to judge according to their circumstances whether a human being born at that time would get the care and upbringing a human being needs for the fulfillment of its nature—directed to preventing war instead— turning the swords into plowshares, improving the quality of life for those born—what a different world there could be.

Reason Versus Emotion

I have attempted to use reason on the "Right to Life" issue. But emotion intensified by deceit, used to buttress the anti-choice position, makes it difficult to convince with reason and facts alone. What better example to demonstrate the strength of emotion completely obliterating reason than war! How easy it should be to see that both sides cannot be right in war, yet religion has encouraged those on both sides to kill each other, as it were, in obedience to God, the one same God.

God is also appealed to in abortion. When it comes to emotion and deceit, I am unable to decide whether those against choice before birth or against choice after birth, who draft adult people to kill in war, aren't the greater offenders. Perhaps because, ironically, they are very much the same people. Consider: right across the map of the world the anti-choice are at one in compelling birth, pro-life. Then they divide off into separate compartments, and become anti-choice, for conscription, the draft, pro-death against each other, against the lives they insisted be born. What an amount of deceit, conditioning or brainwashing is required on different sides to enthuse all to be anti-life, to want to go forth to kill other parents' children.

The deception so necessary for war is not our concern in this treatise, other than to point out the strength of emotion when manipulated by deceit. The pro-lifer for the fetus practices a different form of deceit; the appeal is aimed at stirring up emotions rooted in a different part of our nature than the one stirred up for war. Animals care for their offspring with a combination of tenderness and firmness that would put many humans to shame. See the lion so soft and yielding with his playful cubs. That fierce animal with its adrenal pumping that pounces on the babies of other animals, the enemy, to sustain its young, is one and the same lion. Should the predator show any hesitation or weakness due to consideration for the prey, the prey would escape, the cubs would die, the links in the food chain would break down, incurring the termination of the species.

It is that part of our survival mechanism that kicks in for war, and is the source of our exultation in killing them, the enemy. What a high proportion of babies born will kill and be killed by other babies!

The other facet, the love of parents for their young, that soft and tender feeling, is played up on the side of the fetus. The fetus is portrayed as a cute little baby (not as a child molester, murderer, possible suicide, or a Hitler), even with thoughts of a fairly advanced age, that show absolutely no resemblance to the real fetuses I found on the toilet seat. There are many many examples of well-meaning deception to buttress the anti-choice argument. Allow me to refer to one, a fiction, as if it were real. Some thirty college students showed how hearing the narration tugs at heartstrings!

Cardinal Stefan Wyszynski of Poland outlined the reflections of a fetus from the moment of the egg and sperm's meeting to the day it was aborted some eleven weeks later. It was a Polish fetus and thought in Polish, of course. The Polish was then translated into English, with something, we may assume, being lost in the translation. The last words of the eleven-week-old Polish fetus were, "Today my mother killed me."

How can reason and truth be used against such methods of persuasion? With all due disrespect to the cardinal and his translator, I suggest that all the billions of miscarriages could just as well have ended with, "Today God killed me." Were the fetus as the cardinal suggests, what a monster his

God would be, Hitler only a faint imitator, but perhaps, adequate to make him a candidate for sainthood. Really, a little thought on our part should tell us that the fetus has no such thoughts, nor such ability to think until many years after birth, and then only if given a suitable upbringing. It is pure fiction to impute such mentation to a fetus.

But what is most real, and not infrequent, are the couples that long for a baby, making all sorts of preparation down to even choosing the name, buying baby clothes, furniture, and decorating the room, only to have their hopes dashed by a miscarriage. Shall we aver that God killed the baby they wanted to love and care for? I would not, of course. The reader may wish to recall my consideration of the billions, quintillions of miscarriages earlier, as an indication of how God values an actual fetus.

Many hypothetical people are created by anti-choice people. These "could have beens" always manifest only positive values. The truth is we don't know how any might develop. Just today I learned of an eighteen-year-old who put a gun to his own head. Only a few days previously, a policeman in New York was the eighth this year to have committed suicide. He was a twenty-four-year-old, and only three months married. My second next-door neighbor committed suicide, one of my former classmates, possibly more than one close relative and many others I have known took their own lives. And I have just listened to a person formerly so happy to have beaten the odds and been born, now wishing her birth had never taken place.

Pick up the newspaper on any one day and view all the tragedies reported. And we are not including the millions of killers and killed in wars, natural disasters and horrible disease, not to mention the Hitlers, Bushes, or Husseins.

I have observed babies and kittens and puppies after being born; it would be difficult to infer from their behavior any great difference in their early stages of consciousness.

Definitely, a fetus does not think, not in Polish nor English, nor any other language. It would be reasonable to assume that a fetus in the early stages has as much thought process as a tomato, and were it to express itself, it would be close to the idiom tomatoes use. Yet people fall for it. Otherwise, why engage in such drivel?

It is normal to bring joy with birth and leave sorrow with death. We grow up, develop, and interrelate with other people. Our joys and sorrows are wrapped up with others. With the fetus, no relationship is established. Undoubtedly, and thankfully, miscarriages do bring disappointment, often great depression. Such pain is a measure of the want and need in the would-be parents for the child, that ideally no child born should lack. But nature, or God, determines otherwise. In the case of the wanted child, God or nature says no; for the unwanted child, society says, yes.

With those actually born, the relationship becomes totally different. Earlier in this book I referred to a friend who was so down after her miscarriage until I spoke with her. The one she did have and would not have had, but for the miscarriage, became her love, which were she to lose now, in either peace or war, would leave a wound lasting to the grave. The miscarriage is a thing of the past.

My wife and I endured three of nature's abortions. As we had twins instead of one miscarriage, it is possible that we lost more than three fetuses. Had we lost one of them after birth, the pain would have been great, and more or less, depending on the time and relationship reached. The pain resulting from the loss of my two-year and nine-month-old brother is, after sixty years, still with me. As I write, it is reported that three hundred people turned out to mourn at the funeral of an eight-month-old tragically killed, the same number that mourned for my two friends lost in war.

One of the twins, my delightful daughter, was so glad to be alive and so selfish, that she expressed delight that we had suffered the miscarriage that permitted her to be conceived and born. Another of my daughters complained that she did not ask to be born. But she has probably forgiven us, as she herself has with full intention conceived and given birth. How much my wife and I are joyfully occupied with our grandchild.

When she was a little over a year old, my beloved sister died, taking much of me with her to the grave. I reflected that I would hate to have to decide between my sister and my granddaughter. Yet that grandchild would not exist at all had not my daughter and her husband decided to defer the pregnancy, but not defer it any further.

Please, good people, let's away with emotion, especially emotional deceit. My existing four children are much of my life. The three nature aborted, not at all. Only actual people form connections with other actual people. Those that never see the light of day, all those billions to infinity, whether conceived or not conceived, aborted or miscarried, or who died in the womb because of the would-be mother's death due to accident, execution, war, or natural causes such as earthquake, flood and famine—called acts of God—make no lasting impact. A possible individual impinges on nobody, develops no relationships.

During World War II, the whole village of Carrigaline, at the time some three hundred souls, were awaiting the return of the much-liked Mossey Dennehy from the war. Everyone knew that a new bed had been bought for him. In the midst of all the joyful anticipation came the numbing news: he was lost at sea. Tommy Harrington was lost as well. The whole village was plunged into sorrow. In all my years, all the miscarriages and abortions put together could not compare with that one loss of two people with whom we all related. We may speculate on the extent of the pain caused by the loss of eight uncles of one lady I knew, all killed in World War I.

My own life has been particularly painful. I would surely be terrified had I to live it over again. Perhaps, selfishly, had I the choice, I would choose not to have been born, but I would not have been able to enjoy my nonexistence, as I did not in all the eons I did not exist.

The Right of the Possible

Let us make a quick review of the individual from what leads up to its conception, conception being the point currently considered appropriate for social interference to begin, and continuing on until death, when for the most part social involvement ends, but not a moment before, suicide being against state law.

The individual in the realm of the possible is one of a countless number. The single sperm from one ejaculation that survives to impregnate the egg is by itself one of a number that boggles the mind. Add to them all the sperm lost by that one individual over a lifetime, enough to populate the earth many times over. What would it be to the power of, if all sperm entered an egg? Perhaps modern math not depending on zeros, no matter how tiny which would stretch around the world, can represent the number, but the imagination falls far short. And each one of these sperm could have combined with any one of all the eggs in existence, continuing on down the ages, giving conception to particular possible individuals, a number so vast that I doubt very much that even modern math serviced with all current electronic equipment could furnish an estimate. But out of all those well-nigh infinite possibilities, some particular conceptions do occur. What chance led to my own conception over seventy years ago I know not; but telling a young girl from Ireland in Kennedy International (Idlewild) what to do with the slice of lemon served with her tea—to squeeze it—was the chance link in the chain of events which led to the existence of my four children. Their right to be conceived had the same validity as the countless number not conceived. Whence their right to be born?

Let us pause for a moment on the meaning of right in this context. A sperm without right to impregnate meets an egg without right to be impregnated. But as soon as they have met, the right to be born exists. Whence the right? Did the sperm and ovum give it to each other? That particular combination had the same right as countless others a second before. So, to reiterate, whence the right? Does society give the right or recognize an inherent right, as well as society's own duty to see that the right is exercised against the wishes of the couple directly involved?

The right to birth is reminiscent of the rights and powers of elected rulers, which pass above and beyond the rights and powers of those who elect them. After election, rulers become endowed with an added charisma from on high. Even Albert Reynolds, the Irish ex-prime minister, laid claim to the divine dimension.

The right-to-life concept manifests a similar pre-democratic mind-set. Neither the parents nor the semen and the ovum give the right; it is bestowed from on high. Such an approach is no more, in practice, than the old teaching, already refuted, that God issues a soul at the precise moment of impregnation. That belief may not be used as the grounds for justification, but it surely is responsible for the mind-set, just as strongly as the mind-set resulting from the inheritance of divine right kingship has proved much too strong for real democracy.

How does society recognize the right in the fetus? By intuition? And whence is derived the right and/or duty to impose on the couple?, and furthermore, use the particular association, the state, as an instrument in its enforcement? Or, in all honesty are we cornered, and have to fall back on an appeal to a God-given right?

But how justify that base as God denies through miscarriages the right He grants to so many billions? Nobody has suggested that when Christ wrote with his finger on the ground in defense of the woman taken in adultery, that he wrote of the right to life of her unborn. Nor did it motivate those who with Judah were stoning his daughter-in-law to death after her pregnancy became manifest; it was the ring revealing that Judah was the impregnator that saved the mother and twins.

Nor did I ever hear of a conception being the grounds to defer a woman's execution in either the world of Islam or Catholicism. What if Joan of Arc had been pregnant! And what about witches! As for war, we've come to grips with killing the innocent: women, children and the aged, but what about the innocent in the womb! How many were lost in Hiroshima, Dresden, in the wars of the twentieth century alone, not forgetting the glory of Desert Storm? Even President Clinton thought we should all feel good about his ordering the thirty-thousand-pound bombing of Baghdad, making God so happy.

By our actions we deny any absolute right in the fetus. Right can only be what God grants in His infinite wisdom, not forgetting His infinite goodness. Then, the right is not an absolute right inherent in the fetus. It is based on power. God gives and God has the right—equals Power—to take it away. The same right that denies the choice of death to the suffering incurably ill. The right is not inherent in the person or the fetus; the right is in God. With Him lies the power, not only of creating the right in the fetus, but also of creating the duty for the rest of society to strive to ensure that the Divine right to terminate is not usurped. (But it is all right, to counter the Divine will in natural disasters. And, of course, the duty in war to take the lives under orders of those who don't want to die merits the highest Divine award.)

If the duty is not an option, a further most difficult ethical problem arises. What is the extent to which the right-to-lifers should go to facilitate birth?—should they kill the abortion doctor as has been done and recommended or—see that all pregnant women have the best care available to ensure healthy babies and safe deliveries, or forbid smoking the world over, burn tobacco crops because it is unhealthy for those unborn! To designate abortion as legal murder, as many strive to do, carries logically with it the inference that a miscarriage resulting from neglect is manslaughter.

To focus more clearly on the implied ramifications of the right to life, let us review the evolution of the fetus from conception on, not just to birth, but continuing life after birth.

The fetus begins with a sort of vegetative life, evolves through a fish stage, shading off into animal. Once born it manifests a consciousness no higher than other mammal babies. Gradually it distinguishes itself from the offspring of other species. But experience demonstrates that it is upbringing that largely determines what the adult individual will become. This is evidenced not only by the learning of language, general culture and characteristics, but even the development of reason itself that is commonly held to be what sets humans apart from the brute kingdom.

It is now certain that some animals educated in a human environment manifest characteristics hitherto considered human, whereas humans deprived of human social contact or worse, exposed only to animal upbringing in their early years, advanced little beyond the animal stage, despite protracted efforts at human rehabilitation.

When people are deprived of human upbringing, they manifest little of human traits. The children of slum people are slum people; the children of primitive people are primitive unless raised in a different environment than their parents. Even children raised in the wilds during their early formative years respond only faintly to civilizing influences. Those brought up by wolves manifest the ways of wolves. A girl so raised up to her eighth year before being introduced to civilization continued to go on all fours, resisted wearing clothing, could see better at night than in daylight, and never slept beyond midnight. She ate wolf fashion; ate carrion and drove away vultures and crows so she could have it. Her sense of sound and smell were far more acute than those brought up in human society. She was able to smell a dead chicken eighty yards away.

In contrast, the boy who spent all of a long period of his young life in a cellar, experiencing neither night nor day, and with almost no human or animal contact, was very poor in his use of all senses. Despite intensive efforts, neither of those beings attained in human terms what is normal for a three-year-old brought up in an average social setting. The young man, known as Kasper Hauser, who had experienced some human contact from his "jailer," did learn to speak some words. He left us some poignant ones. After the first attempt at his assassination—by humans—from which although gravely wounded, he recovered, he uttered, "You should have first killed me before I understood what it is to live." The second assassination attempt did kill him.

Tarzan makes entertaining fiction, but could not be true. Perhaps the creation has an edge on the Polish fetus, whose thoughts were chronicled by Cardinal Wyszynski and translated for the pages of *America.*

By such reflections we should feel chastened, that no matter what our genetic inheritance—the particular combination of chromosomes that determines our individuality, making each of us who we are and no other—it is nevertheless our upbringing that determines so much what we become, even to the very extent of being participating members of the human race, whom to murder in war and for whom.

With such an expose of what is essential to become human

after birth, how can people who assume responsibility for insisting on birth deny any responsibility for insuring a worthwhile existence to those born? In fact, often it's the very same people who resent having to contribute in taxes to the raising of those born to single mothers. But they enter the picture again at a later date, to force the surviving person to lay his life on the line in taking the lives of other survivors.

The social milieu in which we develop after birth is analogous to our development before birth. Without the stimulus of human culture, we do not realize much if any of our potential as human beings. It should be safe to infer from experience that it is by and through society that we grow to develop a moral sense, to have a conscience. It was noted of those raised outside human society that any sense of justice was lacking. It is our immediate associates with whom we develop an affinity and identity, who form ours.

Different groups have a different morality or customs which set them apart from each other, the morals of one seeming strange to the others. That strangeness or otherness contributes to defining us, separating us from them. Unfortunately, often this distinction extends beyond mere custom; it becomes right and wrong, good and bad. We are right and good and they are wrong and bad. The values assimilated become the values of right and wrong for the individual conscience within his group.

But then something quite extraordinary may occur. An individual conscience formed by society can find itself at odds with the general conscience of the group; it can rise above the group and raise its identity to that of membership in the whole human race and refuse to be part of killing fellow humans on order by the group. If he does experience the necessity to kill, it is on his conscience alone, his moral responsibility and not the depravity of blind obedience. His general conscience: "Thou shalt not kill a fellow human";

their conscience: "Thou shalt kill your fellow humans" (they are our enemies). It is not uncommon for the humanist, who does not insist on any inherent right to be born, to find himself at odds in his refusal to kill his fellows by those who saw it as their duty that the killers and those to be killed have life in the first place.

Strange that apart from human contact, the individual is devoid of conscience; with human contact, he can develop a conscience of a higher level than that of the group that formed it.

How it is that an individual conscience can become at variance with the group that formed it will not be addressed in this study. But the variance is crucial, and the unwillingness of each group to accept readily the conscientious maverick in its midst, while at the same time affirming vociferously the absolute nature of the individual conscience, must score high on the scale of human contradiction.

Surely, to become fully human is the highest stage of the evolution that began with conception. Is it not more important to reach the highest point of life than to begin life? As life through the various stages is best considered a continuum, its culmination and perfection is reached when it leaves the tribe behind and reaches the human level. Each day for my granddaughter is a new day, a new creation, and not without input from me—a change in the continuum.

Let us pause in our study of the right to life. It is the right to human life, to the full responsibility of a human being, that is the object of our study, not a heart beating or lungs breathing. Should we equate "human being," not from the potential to be human, nor from the joining of the sperm and egg, nor the beating heart or even birth itself, but with the full realization of what it is to be human, the stages to full humanity can be considered as broadly threefold. First, the gestation period within the womb; second, the period within the group in which very gradually we are formed by our immediate environment, even to the use of our senses, and up to the limit of group identity and maximum loyalty; third, when the individual embraces human values, experiences himself as a member of the human race, takes full responsibility for his own life and actions, justifying nothing by an appeal to obeying orders.

Perhaps the second period should be divided into two. I suggest a subdivision rather than two separate stages, to reflect the analogy with the gestation period within the womb—when the evolution from the initial union of the seed and egg through the vegetative, fish, and animal stage takes place before life outside the womb begins—and the group conscience starts to develop.

The reader may prefer to consider the period from birth to what has been called the age of reason (traditionally accepted as approximately seven years) as a very different stage, as it were, the passage from animal to human, corresponding to the definition of human as rational animal. I choose to consider the period of tribal formation as one complete gestation period, because the age of reason is obviously rooted in tribal values. So I view that whole period as a second gestation period.

This is the total span—that which makes the Jew and the Nazi, the Muslim, the Catholic, the Protestant, and the Hindu, the Irish, the English, the Iraqi, the American, who killed in Hebron and who was killed, who killed in Belfast and who was killed. That is the period that makes the individual what defines him, that answers the question, what are you?

Finally the third stage is when—by what may be classified as an ethical leap from the tribe and nation, the sovereign individual, as a member of the whole human race, takes full responsibility for his life and actions—a human being is born. Now the question is, *who* are you?

For him, the right to life is the right to the full life of the autonomous, responsible individual. No one should choose less. And above all, not choose life for one who will be obliged to give it up later in response to the tribal madness that will force him to kill.

Every human being should be pro-life in general. In particular, who best to guarantee a good life than the primary lovers, the parents?

If it is accepted that the right to life should be equated with the right to the good life, the obverse is necessarily true, the right not to have life, when a bad life can be anticipated. Because of the right not to be born with strikes against one, the strongest argument can be made for public funding of abortions for the poor. Much less is it the right of the parent to choose than the right of the fetus not to be born. The old right-to-lifer, claimed to speak for the helpless fetus that could not speak for itself. However, the new right-to-lifer, must speak for the helpless fetus' right not to be born unless it is reasonable to anticipate a good life for it. How many are there who will be born, and wish they never were, some who will be driven in desperation to attempt to take their own lives, not to mention the lives they will be compelled to take.

We need not turn to famine-stricken countries to view human misery. Currently in the land of liberty a child is abused or neglected every thirteen seconds, every day 1,234 run away from home, while 100,000 have no home to go to. And Washington has estimated that all told, the number of homeless people has reached seven million. Is it outrageous to suggest that had they foreseen their lot, many would choose not to be born? Who is to speak for them? Could they have a right not to be born? And is it absurd to concede that some recognize it as a duty to prevent such births, acknowledge the right not to be born to a life of misery? And at the very least, what gives others the right to insist that they are? There are those who aver the right to life and those who advance the right to choose, but who proposes the right not to be born to a life of misery?

To hasten that day, the day in which life becomes synonymous with the full life that begins at the moment of conception, and the whole process is understood as one continuum which continues developing through birth and beyond the tribe to full personality as a human being—who will refuse, at the cost of his own life if necessary, to take the life of another on command—I suggest a change in nomenclature to reflect the changed concepts.

Those now using the **"right-to-life"** label will be named for that stage in the continuum, birth, which is their active concern, and called ***"right to birth."*** Those holding that, if possible, all born should have a reasonable chance of a full life, with, as things now stand, the would-be parents being the major factor in assuring that life, will claim the appellation **"right to life."**

Reality Versus Faith

Once democracy is established as our guide to life, the state will be recognized as a unit of people organized under a representative body to protect and facilitate economic well-being in this life; it will, then, become clear that otherworldly considerations are no business of state.

While acknowledging that the state is a worldly organization for the well-being of its members and may not be the means to impose on the individual member's conscience, unless the individual's conscience challenges the well-being of others, nevertheless, the function of aiding the free exercise of conscience could be envisioned as a legitimate field of government involvement. What higher property of a person than conscience!

Here a face-off between this world and the next may well be anticipated. The state can permit, even facilitate the free exercise of conscience, yet must defend itself if it is threatened by such exercise. The state has to walk the fine line between defending the free exercise of individual conscience and protecting other members from the consequences of such exercise when their safety is involved.

No such subtleties had to perturb the minds of nondemocratic communities, especially religiously dominated ones. There was only one conscience—theirs. When societies for the next life experienced a challenge to the means to life's purpose by an "erring" conscience, no balancing act was sought. The simple solution—execution.

Now, a totally new situation is upon us; we may view it as difference in kind rather than degree: world resources are limited, some economic units more so than others, while all indications are that the population is on a constant increase. So, it is not just between individuals, families, and states that conflicts are to be reconciled, but the whole world is vitally involved. The scenario has moved: the right to the possibility of a good life is not inseparable from those actually in existence being threatened by overpopulation. Societies' right to self-defense comes into play. Not only, then, may the family, the would-be parents, be subject to state control in the matter of births, but to world population control as well.

But, in this, let us beware not to confuse the economic grounds for state and world control with either state or world sovereignty. Unfortunately, the compromises leading up to the Cairo Conference, points to a noninterference by the U.N. with the sovereignty of individual political units, confusing nondemocratic sovereignty in morals with the democratic responsibility of each economic unit to confine its population within its ability to provide.

Without, at this time, making any judgment as to the threat of overpopulation, we must acknowledge its possibility. It is not when the actuality is imminent or upon us that we should face the issue, but now, while we may have some breathing space. Having accepted that the reasonable expectation of a good life is the condition for life being bestowed, and that parents are the best guarantee and judge if the good life can be anticipated, nevertheless there is a much wider question that may override the judgments of parents. Whereas particular parents may judge that resources for the good life for their offspring exist, there may be very many parents looking to the same resources, resulting in competition and limitation even with those already born. Who then is to decide on that fundamental issue? It must be by those already in existence. It would have to be the wider communities of which families are a part, if not the world at large, that estimates the population that can be supported.

Had the New World not been discovered, Europe would have been unable to feed its population by the end of the nineteenth century. It was relieved not only by large-scale emigration, but by food imports from the new virgin lands. But now that we have run out of world, what is to be done as mounting population pressure and dwindling resources combine to threaten the good life of those already born and deny a reasonable expectancy of such to future generations? Who is in a position to understand the problem, and who is in a position to recommend, even enforce, if necessary, the solution?

Representatives may meet on a worldwide basis, but who is to enforce, or take on the responsibility? There is no world government. The highest units, the highest economic units with governments empowered to enforce, are states. Who else, then, is to assume the responsibility? It must be for each state to keep its own house in order. To use the analogy with a lifeboat: should one boat take on more than it can support, it may not pass its lack of decision onto another and threaten the other's survival. So if a particular society fails in its responsibility to limit population growth, why should it be permitted to export its surplus to a state that has shouldered its responsibility? If the rest of the world must acquiesce in the sovereignty of each state, it should not have to pick up the tabs, or to change the metaphor—let each economic unit stew in its own juice.

Clearly, a major standoff can be envisioned between those who conceive this world as a passageway to the next, in a life hereafter, the quality of this life being of small moment, and those who assert the importance of this life, for some, the only life.

At the outset of this work, we thought we had reconciled the opposing sides by showing that the principles of one were not in conflict with those of the other. By such a presentation it was hoped that the consciences of one side could be reconciled with those of the other, that society at large, church and state, could safely take up a neutral position, and let the would-be parents make the decision; that nobody was for compelling abortion.

Population excess was not included in our study. Now, of course, population control can be envisioned, possibly by a world body to which states delegate authority, and whose directives the states accept as binding. But whether the edicts come from a world body or sovereign states, it must ultimately be through the particular families that they are observed. The freedom of the family is not absolute, but conditional. The right of those born to the good life may no longer be the decision of each family. Without questioning the competency of the parents to make a short-term decision about their own ability to provide for their offspring, the decision cannot be exclusively the parents'. The rights of all parents in matters of procreation must be reconciled when conflicts of interest arise. Coordination at a state and world level can be anticipated.

If the government in China did not take drastic steps to limit its population, the consequences could be horrendous not only for China, but also for the rest of the world, perhaps Australia most. Think of the nightmare if China were fundamentalist Islamic like Bangladesh, already stricken with famine and forbidden participation in the population conference in Cairo. Or if China were Catholic! Not even allowed artificial contraception—even the lotus foot?

Associations and individuals for a life hereafter, opt to usher people through this life—"Life," said St. Theresa of Avila, "is like a night in a wayside inn on the road home"—will not lightly acquiesce in a system that places such emphasis on the quality rather than the quantity of life. So-called pro-lifers may decry all they like the murders of pro-abortion people, but there is no better witness to the logic of such actions than the churches themselves; when the power lay with them, murder in such issues was the order of the day.

For this-world people, once it is accepted that there is no more living space left, each unit must be responsible for limiting its own population. Just as each family should not exceed its own ability to provide, so must each state confine its population growth to its own resources, with, we may anticipate, some input from the universe at large.

Should a particular sovereign unit fail in its responsibility, do those who are responsible have to open their doors to the improvident and consequently ration themselves?

If we justify war, and kill millions and destroy vast areas in the cause of self-defense and property, surely each economic unit has a right and duty to control its own population. Nor as humans can any be indifferent to people in other units giving birth into a world or unit that promises misery for them and/or hardship for those already in existence.

Now the awesome question arises, must the democracies fall back on the same expedient as authoritarian regimes, churches, and fundamentalists? For example, when you can't convince, destroy? The churches, seeing the heretic as the enemy of the next world, in their solicitude for others, logically, executed him. Is there no other option but for the democratic states to imitate the churches?

What can be done in self-defense to counteract the powerful moral persuasion of such revered figures as Pope John Paul II and Mother Teresa?—people very likely no less noble and dedicated than many other witnesses to principle, such as Giordano Bruno and Michael Servitus, both martyred at the stake; the former for his mundane views of the cosmos, the latter for his religious views? The physician had escaped the frying pan of the Roman Catholic Inquisition only to fall into the fire of Calvinist Protestant Geneva.

Cannot the consequences of the freedom of speech of Pope John Paul II vastly outweigh granting freedom of speech to terrorists or crying fire in a crowded theater? The church's solution was to set fire to the challenging speaker.

Whatever steps this world takes to protect itself by population control; whatever means it uses to confine the enemy; time may not be on its side. States will not be faced with just boat people fleeing from dictators hammering on our doors for political asylum, but boat people fleeing starvation, begging for food.

I had some hesitation as to the immediate necessity of the foregoing pages, but as I opened today's *Bergen Record,* August 24, 1994, I read of overpopulation being referred to as a myth. Vernon Walters, President Reagan's U.N. ambassador, declared that world population was no business of the U.N's: "The United Nations is not a religious body organized to express moral values," he said. In that short statement, the issue is succinctly joined. Were it just a moral issue, I could not agree more. The reader is well aware how much of my efforts have been subjected to taking morality altogether out of state auspices, so *a fortiori* out of empire, of nations united, or even world government. But it is not simple morality such as the veiling of faces in Cairo or whether states should get involved with sex and the "missionary position." Self-defense from morality is the kernel. The gauntlet is thrown down between this world and the next.

Well, indeed, it may be that the world could, if organized, marshalled, and compelled by an all-wise dictator, provide basic sustenance for a much larger population. Even if it were thought desirable, there is no such world governor. What we do have are sovereign nations, whose business is economic, uniting with one another for economic and not moral reasons. Will the United Nations be able to impose on any nation, or compel it to open its door? And should it?

What the conference of over 160 nations is proposing is a blueprint of voluntary ways to curb world population and integrate developmental and population strategies. Mother Teresa wants the population conference to offer care for all unwanted babies, possibly an ideal Marxist solution if we had a Marxist world, but although naive, an improvement on Mr. Walters who sees it purely as a moral issue. "From all according to ability, to each according to need," said the idealist Marx. Communism has already failed.

In the world as it is, are those who responsibly limit population, either within the family, location, or nation, according to their ability to provide, then to open their doors and ration themselves for the improvident? In an analogy with the wise and foolish virgins, who if they shared their oil could all have ended up in darkness, let those who insist on overpopulation, enjoy the benefits and/or suffer the consequences.

Muslim and Catholic forces have joined together to bring pressure to bear on the Cairo Conference. If Islamic Bangladesh, with its devastating famine in recent times, or Catholic Ireland, insist on using otherworldly values, then let them accept the consequences and not export them to those more provident than they.

On the same page of the newspaper referred to above, we read of Israel's fear that millions of people will try to escape Third World poverty by claiming Jewish ancestry. Without holding any brief for the proposal of Uri Gordon, head of the immigration department of the Jewish Agency, to limit immigration to those with a Jewish parent— shades of a little reverse discrimination—I, nevertheless, do not see how Israel or any country is obliged, much less should be compelled, to give free entry to all who come. Surely those who labored so hard to build up an economy, should not be compelled to give the fruit of their labor to others.

Demography is not my field. It is not for me to make the decisions that the warnings on world overpopulation are well-founded, or if wildlife should be pushed off the globe to make way for humans, or if environmental changes endanger the survival of the planet earth, or what validity in the overall scheme of values should be given to theological doctrine: the urgency to replace fallen angels in a depopulated heaven, conforming to a theological sexuality, or other reason. I want to point out to those for whom the value of this world is to function as a gestation period to the next, that the conflict between both worlds could be a contest to the death. This is not the reconciliation of the medieval problem of faith and reason that Aquinas undertook, the faith of believers being threatened. That was purely another world problem. The present struggle is between two different worlds, the world of experience and the world of faith, each considering the other a threat to itself.

The bottom line is that secular bodies are ill equipped to defend themselves from a morality that threatens to destroy them. This is not an isolated or limited case such as the nine hundred induced to take poisoned Kool-Aid by Jim Jones, or David Koresh's Waco inferno giving birth to heaven, or Mary Tudor's three hundred at Smithfield, or Cromwell's three thousand at Drogheda, in addition to the massacre of St. Bartholomew, even the hundred million in twentieth-century wars. This threat is to the whole world, and by a mighty force. How are the troops to storm the compound?

The reader will recall that in our removal of religion and morality from the sphere of democratic government, we adamantly asserted the freedom of moral and religious values, not just those pertaining to abortion, being promulgated worldwide without aid or hindrance. But what if the exercise of such freedom on a worldwide basis could prove the enemy of the world, and, of course, democracy with it!

Rights cannot be absolute rights if they can be in conflict, whether the limitation is expressed in terms of shouting "fire" in a crowded theater, or "your freedom to swing your arm ends where my nose begins."

The first proponent of democracy, John Locke, understood the democratic state to be an association of people who agree to band together for the defense of their lives and property. And the more liberal thinker, John Stewart Mill, reduced all valid interference with the freedom of an adult by society to just one issue. That issue—self-defense.

No one can be so irrational as to permit a freedom that will lead to one's own destruction.

In the earlier part of this writing, we separated the state secular powers from the moral sphere. By denying religious powers the right to use the state to inhibit the free exercise of the individual conscience, moral persuasion by a state, even on a worldwide basis, was encouraged.

The separation of church and state—the state agreeing not to hinder the free exercise of religion or individual morality; the religious and the moralists agreeing to desist from using the state to impose their religious and moral ways—was our resolution to such conflicts as contraception, divorce, and abortion, or stamping out celibacy.

But when the individual conscience or mass conscience formed by otherworldly values becomes a challenge to the secular power, all bets are off. The secular power must defend itself with the means at its disposal, and not just from individual murders, but from a way of life that threatens the whole raison d'etre of the state. Even if events in Waco were badly managed, surely the right, even duty, to interfere cannot be denied.

Education should be the answer, but how do we reconcile two diametrically opposed value systems, each based on a different world? We've had enough troubles between East and West. Japan didn't play cricket. They bombed first and declared war afterwards.

Time Is of the Essence

At the outset, the invitation to the open-minded was to consider first the spiritual nature of the soul, and secondly, God's or Nature's prodigality with miscarriages, to which could more appositely be applied the Pope's denunciation of abortion as "a project of systematic death of the unborn." Miscarriages are by God. We used nature's systematic miscarriages as proof that we were not dealing with human beings, thereby removing abortion from public involvement.

Then, having crested the first wave, a much more difficult task was undertaken, to remove all such moral issues from democratic state jurisdiction. After those two we thought we could rest, but a direct clash has arisen between those who want to limit population to the needs of this world and those in a hurry to populate the next world by means of this.

In an attempt to crest the third wave, I beg the reader to reflect on the nature of time and eternity: what do theologians teach about God's relationship, or lack of relationship, to time?

According to the subtlety of theologians, God is not in time. The Creator did not exist from eternity; He is. There is no past and future with Him. Time is of this world. It is a facet of material creation that it can have its duration measured and counted, when there is someone to measure and count. There is no, or was no "when" of the beginning of the universe. God was not from all eternity thinking of creating the world. It is as meaningless to ask if God could have created the universe at an earlier or later time, a different time, as it would be to ask if He could have put it in a different place. For there is no time and no place apart from the universe. Time and place are only with the universe, "when" and "where" being aspects of it.

The metaphysician, Immanuel Kant, taught that time and space demand a time/space mind to categorize them as we do. But absolutely, the phenomena of time and space are not the most real. Time and space are subject to the categories of the human mind to be known, to be experienced. Ontologically that is not how they are. As St. Thomas Aquinas expressed it: "Things in time and space are known according to the mode of the knower." But God knows what really is, the noumena, without extension or succession. All existence is *tota simul.*

For God there is no rush to make up the numbers for heaven; they are already there, or here.

For those unfamiliar with such concepts and accustomed to thinking in cosmological terms, let us first think of the time from all eternity that elapsed before God eventually did it. He had decided from all eternity when—then consider all the time since time began, billions of years, even since life began, or just human life. The evidence is that something approaching human life existed some thirty to forty million years ago. But to make our point, it is not necessary to go back that far, not even to the millennia of recorded history. After the age of Napoleon, only as recently as 1830, the world population had reached one billion—a figure now far surpassed by China alone. By the time of my birth in 1924, the population had almost doubled, and reached nearly two billion. Now, seventy years later, it is almost six billion.

Consider, there were people alive in this writer's lifetime who had lived in a world whose total population was less than China's is today. What a chastening thought!

What patience! What a long time God waited for the population explosion, although modified slightly by the total war and natural disasters to occur! I suggest, as I did with abortions as imitations of nature's miscarriages, that we also imitate the Divine patience and exercise our responsibility to guard His universe from the overpopulation that could lead to its destruction.

But let those unaffected by the metaphysics of time or uninfluenced by its slow cosmology, at least try to understand that the people for this world must protect themselves and the earth for future generations, from overpopulation, and its attendant violence and cholera and plague that knows no bounds.

The world has experienced religious wars, next-life wars, and dynastic, this-life wars; a religious war turning into dynastic, the Thirty Years' War; and a war pure and simply dynastic with a veneer of religion fought between William III of Orange against the Catholic James II, the Catholic Emperor and the Pope fighting with William. But for the very first time is the struggle between this world and the next. How is it to be fought? History is replete with the methods of otherworld bodies.

The answer of religions, especially Catholic and Islamic to what was conceived as a threat to God's world, was to destroy the enemy, each other, before they learned to share this world, although still not in the Balkans. With the Christian Crusades, those who died in the killing were promised instant paradise. No complaints on breach of promise were lodged.

Is there no other solution now? Or can we take a leaf from the book of the superpowers of yesteryear—coexist? Ah, but there's the rub, existence is at stake. Is it to be this life or the next? Could we make a division? As after the Peace of Augsburg, the people who wanted a particular religion went to live in areas where their religion prevailed. That solution, though far from ideal, was thought preferable to mutual destruction. Education failing, do we have a better solution? Create this-world and next-world zones—as formerly in Berlin, then, at least part will survive! Really not feasible: epidemic and population pressure cannot be isolated. There are no confining walls.

This world must protect itself from suicide squads, no matter what form they take. As Nobel-laureate, physicist Henry Kendall of M.I.T. observed, "If we don't control the population with justice, humanity, and mercy, it will be done for us by nature—brutally." Some may choose to substitute "God" for "nature." Quoted in *Time,* September 5, 1994.

There is a certain irony if in their efforts to control population, it is this-world people who protect human habitation and enable it to continue, insuring in the long run a greater population, while God's people will kill the goose that lays the golden egg.

Epilogue—
Nancy Reagan, democrat

Shortly after submitting this book for publication, four United States ex-first ladies broke silence, admitting they were pro-choice. If I had any remaining doubt as to the need for this publication, it was removed not only by the confusion manifested in the reaction to the announcement, but also by Mrs. Reagan's inability to classify her standing.

The reader will recall the distinction made earlier in the book: values that the individual considers universal and as such must be free to promulgate, but using moral pressure only, not legal. We sought a "principle whereby a *modus vivendi* or coexistence can prevail between diametrically opposed values, so that we readily accept that we will not seek the strong arm of the state to enforce our certitude, but we will confine ourselves to moral pressure."

That principle we saw to be democracy. Mrs. Reagan in being personally against abortion, but not using the government to support or enforce her views, permitting choice to others, said, "That puts me somewhere in the middle, but I don't know what to call that." Mrs. Reagan, you are a small "d" democrat.

More interesting was the reaction of Colleen Parro, executive director of Phyllis Schlafly's Republican National Coalition for Life! For her, Nancy Reagan's unarticulated democracy reflected an "unclear, ambivalent, inconsistent position." What a long way still to travel on the road to democracy!

Ms. Parro likened Mrs. Reagan's position to "saying I don't believe in slavery, but people have a right to own slaves if they choose." Without going into the tangled history of slavery—indeed I have used the analogy myself in a different context elsewhere with St. Paul's endorsement of the institution—a whole volume could be filled with better analogies. Let's content ourselves with a few, always bearing in mind the precise issue: using the power of government to impose a value some, perhaps a majority, consider absolute or universal.

As Ireland and the U.S. have been the two countries most used in this work as examples of failed "democracies," let's begin with Irish analogies. The law was against not only abortion, but contraception. There is talk of the people deciding whether divorce will be permitted—Mrs. Reagan is in an adulterous union according to Irish law. Would Colleen Parro judge a position "unclear, ambivalent, inconsistent," if one would not divorce or use contraceptive devices oneself, yet allow others to make decisions for themselves? There are, fortunately, quite a few democrats who do allow others to act on their own consciences.

In just a few minutes I jotted down a list of about twenty-five practices that many Americans would not permit for themselves, but would allow to others: from vegetarians who consider it wrong to eat flesh, Hindus who won't eat beef, Moslems, pork, to Islamic veiled faces, all the way down to miniskirts, topless and bottomless beaches. The laws in one country or another have been used to deny choice to individuals in all these areas. Is it inconsistent for those who fully accept these customs to embrace democracy and not use the law to impose their morality on all?

The anger of Eleanor Smeal, president of the Feminist Majority Foundation, at the failure of the former first ladies to speak out when they were in a position to influence abortion policy, is understandable. Theirs was a moral failure.

What a startling phenomenon for a student of democracy who, understanding the right of all people to promulgate their moral position worldwide, without hindrance from government, to learn that our presidents' wives are forbidden to express their views beyond their own residence, and probably bedroom. The President involves himself in what, although a proper issue for human concern, is nevertheless no business of democratic government. The President's consort, in every such nondemocratic involvement, is denied the minimum of moral freedom. Frightening, but logical that the obverse side of the "First Man" insisting on using a power without right, leads of necessity to the First Lady having a right without power. How vital it is to embrace democratic principles to ensure liberty for all—especially in the White House!